AF472167

Note for Librarians: A cataloguing record for this book is available from Library and Archives Canada at www.collectionscanada.ca/amicus/index-e.html
ISBN 1-4120-8664-7

Printed on paper with minimum 30% recycled fibre.
Trafford's print shop runs on "green energy" from solar, wind and other environmentally-friendly power sources.

Offices in Canada, USA, Ireland and UK

Book sales for North America and international:
Trafford Publishing, 6E–2333 Government St.,
Victoria, BC V8T 4P4 CANADA
phone 250 383 6864 (toll-free 1 888 232 4444)
fax 250 383 6804; email to orders@trafford.com
Book sales in Europe:
Trafford Publishing (UK) Limited, 9 Park End Street, 2nd Floor
Oxford, UK OX1 1HH UNITED KINGDOM
phone +44 (0)1865 722 113 (local rate 0845 230 9601)
facsimile +44 (0)1865 722 868; info.uk@trafford.com
Order online at:
trafford.com/06-0420

10 9 8 7 6 5 4 3 2

The Main Ride

by
Karen Belcher

The Main Ride

Chapter 1

If you're not convinced that nothing works like faith, I'll count on God to prove it to you over the next few pages of this book. Biblically speaking, faith is without equal in its effect on our lives because God is without equal and faith is the normative invitation He answers with proof. When you read Ephesians 1:19, He says His incomparably great power for us who believe… is like the working of his might strength.

For every Christian that has heard the gospel message at some point, and chose to believe and receive it, our glorious faith walk will begin with an act of faith that brought us into a relationship with Jesus Christ. But it doesn't end there! Having believe in Him, we are called to continue believing all He came to do and say. Tragically, some who have believed in Christ have believed little of him since. He who began a work in us wants to accomplish far more.

We've talked about belief and continuing to believe. God gave us His word first and foremost to call us into relationship with its Author and our Savior. See 2 Timothy 3:16-17. He is talking about teaching, correcting and training.

I'm going to share with you 5 statements of faith I learned in a Bible Study (Beth Moore) at my church.

1) God is who he says he is
2) God can do what he says he can do
3) I am who God says I am
4) I can do all things through Christ
5) God's word is alive and active in me

So as we go on with this book, ride this ride of faith with me and we will see what we can learn from this.

I love this Bible verse—Hebrews 11:6. It says, "Without faith it is impossible to please God, because anyone who comes to him must believe that he exists and that he rewards those who earnestly seek him." Romans 12:2 tells us God's will is good, pleasing and perfect. It is never degrading, but it is always fulfilling. God is the giver of all good gifts. He wants to shower blessings on you. God wants us to be men and women He can bless.

God's pleasure is the end. Our faith is the means. You and I are invited to believe God. I personally think that God is sometimes willing to reveal Himself dramatically even when we're not actively believing Him to make us still believe and reassure us that he is who he says he is and he can do what he says he can. We have been called to a present-active participle walk of faith.

Faith cannot walk alone. Faith on its own changes nothing. For faith to have life, it must find a powerful object in which to be placed or a powerful person by whom to walk.

We can grow in faith, so as we take this ride of faith together, let's get on and let's see where God is going to take us. Thank goodness our faith also develops; maturing and growing as we continue to walk and ride with God. I am reminded of the verse Psalm 37:3, "Trust (lean on, rely on, and be confident) in the Lord and do good; so shall you dwell idea of feeding on God's faithfulness.

The first thing we have to ask ourselves is does our theology match our reality? Sometimes it does and sometimes it does not. One thing I have learned is that God is pleased when we exercise faith. I have also learned that God is offended when our desire for signs and wonders eclipses our desire for him or becomes a request for God to prove himself. God reads the tablets of our hearts.

I still believe much of what I was taught in those early days of VBS and studying somewhat of the Bible but after seeking God for myself, I've become convinced that He is able and willing to do more than I first imagined. I hold this conviction because He performed the impossible in me. We will never outgrow our need to be taught by others who are wiser and more knowledgeable. The body of Christ would nearly collapse without the gift of teaching.

No matter what our track record of doubt and foolishness has been in the past, we can still give God an opportunity to testify to our faith. You see, it's in Christ that we find out who we are and what we are living for. Long before we first heard of Christ… he had his eye on us, had designs on us for glorious living, part of the overall purpose he is working out in everything and everyone. Look at what God did for Moses. He was a murderer and God turned him into a leader. And a coward named Gideon he turned into a courageous hero. He can do amazing things with anyone's life.

Fear is also something people deal with. Fear is a self-imposed prison that will keep you from becoming what God intends for you to be. Money is also something that drives people where they want to be. The most common myth about money is that having more will make me more secure. It won't. Real security can only be found in that which can never be taken from you—your relationship with Jesus Christ. Then there is that need for approval. They want approval—expectations of parents or spouses or children or teachers or friends to control their lives. Many adults are still trying to earn the approval of unpleasable parents. Then what about peer pressure; always worried by what others might think. Unfortunately, those who follow the crowd usually get lost in it.

I don't know many keys to success, but one key to failure is to try to please everyone. Being controlled by the opinions of others is a guaranteed way to miss God's purposes for your life. Jesus said, "No one can serve two masters" and He's right on that again. Without a purpose, life is trivial, petty and pointless. Knowing your purpose gives real meaning to your life. We were made to have meaning.

Sometimes we feel like failures because your struggling to become something and you don't even know what it is. All I know how to do is to get by. Someday, if I discover my purpose, I'll feel I'm beginning to live. Without God, life has no purpose, and without purpose, life has no meaning. Life has no significance or hope. The greatest tragedy is not death, but life without purpose. Knowing your purpose focuses your life. If you want your life to have impact, focus on it and see what happens. You can be busy without a purpose, but what's the point. Those of us who want everything God has for us, let's keep focused on the goal.

Sometimes you're spending time trying to create a lasting legacy on earth. You want to be remembered when your gone. Yet what ultimately matters most will not be what others say about your life but what God says. You were not put on earth to be remembered. You were put here to prepare for eternity. I keep going back to what the Bible says, "Remember, each of us will stand personally before the judgment seat… Yes, each of us will have to give a personal account to God. Fortunately, God wants us to pass this test so he has given us the questions in advance.

"First, what did you do with my Son, Jesus Christ?" God won't ask about your religious background or doctrinal views. The only thing that will matter is did you accept what Jesus did for you and did you learn to love and trust him? Jesus said, "I am the way and the truth and the life. No one comes to the Father except through me." Second, "What did you do with what I gave you?" All the gifts, talents, opportunities, energy, relationships and resources God gave you. Did you use them for the purposes God made for you? Question to consider, what would my family and friends say is the driving force of my life? What do I want it to be? God has planted eternity in the human heart. (Ecclesiastes 3:11) Surely God would not have created such a being as man to exist only for a day! No, no, man was made for immortality.

So if you think about that, this life on earth is just the dress rehearsal before the real production. It is the practice workout before the actual game. The warm up before it all begins. This life is preparation for the next. The reason we feel we should live forever is that God thoughts and feelings with that desire. One day your life here will be over, but it will not be the end of you. Your earthly body is like a tent but your future body is like a house. While on earth there are so many earthly choices. Eternity offers only two; Heaven or Hell. So if we learn to love and trust God's Son, Jesus, you will be invited to spend the rest of eternity with him.

On the other hand, if you refuse and reject his love, forgiveness and salvation, you will spend eternity apart from God forever. To make the most of your life, you must keep the vision of eternity in your mind and the value of it in your heart. There is far more to life than just here and now. The Bible says, "No mere man has ever seen, heard or even imagined what wonderful things God has ready for those who love the Lord." If your time on earth were all there is to your life, I would suggest you starting living it up immediately. Death is not the end of you. Death is not your termination, but your transition into eternity.

Just try to imagine heaven. Our brains only take us so far. We cannot handle the wonder and greatness of heaven. However, God has given us glimpses in his word. We know right now that God is preparing an eternal home for us. Made to last forever! You are saying to yourself right now, why is she telling me about all this? While I still don't know all the answers, I do know this:

1. God is who he says he is
2. God can do what he says he can do
3. I am who God says I am
4. I can do all things through Christ
5. God's word is alive and active in me and I'm believing God.

Another reason I felt in my heart to share with you this book is that we bring glory to God by telling others about him. God doesn't want his love and purposes kept a secret. Once we know the truth, he expects us to share it with others. This is a great privilege—introducing others to Jesus, helping them discover their purpose and preparing them for their eternal destiny. The Bible says, "As God's grace brings more and more people to Christ… God will receive more and more glory." We were planned for God's pleasure. Anything that we do brings pleasure to God; is an act of worship. Trusting God completely means having faith that he knows what is best for your life.

Think about Noah and how it took 120 years to build the ark. I imagine he faced many discouraging days. With no sign of rain year after year, he was ruthlessly criticized as a crazy man who thinks God speaks to him!! I imagine Noah's children were often embarrassed by the giant ship being built in their front yard. Yet, Noah kept on trusting God. Notice that Noah obeyed completely (no instruction was overlooked) and he obeyed exactly in the way and time God wanted it done. It is no wonder God smiled on Noah.

God smiles when we use our abilities. After flood, God gave Noah these simple instructions: "Be fruitful and increase in number and fill the earth … Everything that lives and moves will be food for you. Just as I gave you green plants, I now give you everything." God was basically saying: It is time to get on with your life! Do the things I designed humans to do. Make love to your spouse, have babies, raise families, plant crops and eat meals. Be humans! This is what I made you to be!

Every human activity, except sin, can be done for God's pleasure if you do it with an attitude of praise. You can wash dishes, work on a car, or even write a book for the glory of God.

God intentionally gifted us differently for his enjoyment. You may be gifted at being musical, athletic, mathematical or a thousand other skills. All these abilities can bring a smile to God's face.

One think that I had to learn was I did not bring

glory or pleasure to God by hiding my abilities or by trying to be someone else. I thought one day I wanted to be a hair dresser. Well, I learned real quick that I was a beauty school drop out because that lasted about three days. It was not God's plan for me to be doing hair. I'm still learning as I take this ride of faith. He is doing amazing things with my life.

Put Jesus Christ in the driver's seat of your life and take your hands off the steering wheel. Don't be afraid; nothing under His control can ever be out of control Mastered by Christ, you can handle anything.

Chapter 2

Becoming a Best Friend of God

Friendship with God is built by sharing all your life experiences with Him. He wants to be included in every activity, every conversation, every problem, and even every thought. Now speaking every thought I ask God to even send me some humor, and at that moment, He sent me some humor. It was about my husband whom I love dearly. He was running in and out of the house while I was trying to have a baby shower with a bunch of women. He was making all kinds of noise with a hammer. I thought I wish he would stop making all that noise. I'm trying to have a baby shower. Then I said to myself, "Lord, send me some humor." About that time my mom leans over to me and shays, "I bet you wish right now he would hit his thumb with a hammer" (Not really.) I asked for humor and that's what I got.

Even in the smallest ways, you can carry on a continuous, open-ended conversation with Him through your day, talking with Him about whatever you are doing or thinking at that moment. "Praying without ceasing" means conversing with God while shopping, driving, working or performing any other everyday tasks. The key to friendship with God is not changing what you do, but changing your attitude toward what you do.

Unbelievers often think Christians obey out of obligation or guilt or fear of punishment, but the opposite is true. Because we have been forgiven and set free, we obey out of love! Jesus said, "I have loved you even as the Father has loved me Remain in my love. When you obey me, you remain in my love, just as I obey my Father and remain in His love. I have told you this so that you will be filled with my joy. Yes, your joy will overflows." The truth is—we are as close to God as we choose to be. Intimate friendship with God is a choice, not an accident.

Your problems are not punishment. They are wake-up calls from a loving God. God is not mad at you. He's mad about you, and He will do whatever it takes to bring you back into fellowship with Him. God told the captives in Babylon,

"When you get serious about find me and want it more than anything else, I'll make sure you won't be disappointed."

Think about Him while you are driving your vehicle. You can determine where you are going. I had a preacher once say, "Just take a right if you are lost and you will be found." Pretty good, huh!"

So if you think about where you are going, you more or less determine your own destiny, right! Again, you are probably saying to yourself, "Why is she telling me this?" Then I think about what Paul said, "I want us to help each other with the faith we have. Your faith will help me, and my faith will help you."

Then I think about when you share your faith sometimes you are persecuted. I think about the Christians who share their faith with a non-Christian. Some are made fun of, despised, even sent to prison. When we try to make Jesus Christ our rock, He can help get us through that persecution. Telling other people about Jesus Christ is a big step. When reading the Bible, we are commanded to do that.

We need to also realize that God is a whole lot

more interested in who we are than in what we do. He is so much more interested in our character than He is in anything else. We are human beings, not human doings. We worry about what career we should choose, and the truth is there are many different careers that could be in God's will for our life, because we will take our character into eternity, but not careers.

Being a Christian, a strong Christian, changes a lot with our everyday life styles. It changes our way of thinking, our life style, and yes! Our relationship. As I continue to grow in my Christian walk, I want relationship with people that want to grow in Christ as well

You know how that old saying goes. There are all kinds of people in the world, different cultures, what we like to eat, what we like to wear, what interests us the most, but from God's point of view, there are really only two kinds of people in the world: saved people and lost people.

Think about if you were in a cave, and you were trying to get out of that cave. You knew you were lost inside, and you just keep on trying to find your way out. When you found your way out, you felt free. You see that's the way Christians feel as they are free, free in Christ.

There is no other life. In Christ there is hope. Once you accept Christ as your savior life changes for you after that. It does not mean life is perfect but it is definitely better. You have struggles in life. When Christ becomes your rock, you can get through them so much easier.

Then I think about John 15- the vine. I am the vine and you are the branches. If I remain in you and you in me, you will bear much fruit. Apart from me you can do nothing. If you remain in me and my words remain in you, ask whatever you wish and it will be given to you. This is to my father's glory that you bear much fruit. Sharing yourselves to be my disciples.

If my life is fruitless, it doesn't matter who praises me, and if my life is fruitful, it doesn't matter who criticizes me.

I guess you could say I am getting out of the boat stepping out on the water just a little! So take the main ride! The main boat—the main flight—the main bus—the main taxi—the main heart—tell us what we feel and God reads the tablets of our hearts. When you accept Christ as your personal savior, life changes for you after that so if you have done that, think about where you will go after this life over and this ride in life will end.

Most people hope to go to heaven, but don't hope that will happen—know that! I believe the way to become a Christian is to do it the way the Bible says to do it. In Acts 2:38, it tells you to repent and be baptized, everyone of you, in the name of Jesus Christ for the forgiveness of your sins and you will receive the gift of the Holy Spirit.

Some people will read this book and understand it all. Other people will read it and not pay any attention to it. Other people will read it, make fun of it, and talk about it in a bad way. I'm a big girl now so I handle all the above. You know why? Because Jesus died on the cross for me and you. They spit on him, whipped him, beat him to death so I can take some heat for Jesus Christ.

I love learning and growing in Christ. It is a big part of my life. I take a Bible class on Thursday at Plum Creek Christian Church, and I love it! I love my church. At Plum Creek Christian Church, we have good leadership. We have people who love the Lord and love teaching, and growing in Christ. At Plum Creek, we have been so blessed. We have a lot of people with strong faith. Early in the book, I talk about a Bible verse I really like, Hebrews 11:6. "Without faith, it is impossible to please God because anyone who comes to Him must believe that He exists and that He rewards those who earnestly seek him."

So let's talk about when this life is over, and you spend it in heaven with Jesus in a perfect place with a perfect person.

Think about that—a perfect place with a perfect person. Why would you not choose that? When I go out of town, which is often, I go to church on Sunday. You know why? Not because I feel like I am made to go. I go because I love to go. I want to die and go to heaven and take as many people with me as I can. I am not a perfect person, no! no! no! The Bible says "Those without sin cast the first stone!"

At Plum Creek, I'm worshiping with over 500 people. I hope and pray it continues to grow and grow and grow. I try to get out every day and I try to plant a seed, Some days I feel like I planted a seed. Other days I feel like I planted a garden, Then some days I feel like I haven't done anything. I want to plant a seed or a garden and Apollo can water it and God can make it grow and if I plant a garden, that is even better.

Some are saying, "Why is she telling me this or who does she think she is telling me this again." I'm commanded to tell you this. I'm supposed to share this with you, and I want to share this with you. Why? Because I love Christ, and He loves you, too. I know when this life is over, it won't matter why my career was, what my kids did, what husband did, but what will matter is what I did for God's Son. So every time I walk out my door, I think about my life and what I have done to tell others about Christ. I don't want to keep that secret so I pray God will put people in my life that I can share with and if they are a Christian, we have a bond we can talk about and share together. I believe that people come into your life for a reason. Everything happens for a reason. My oldest son, for example, thought he was going to college in Bowling Green, Kentucky, but the Lord had different plans for him. Now, he is at a college in Nashville, Tennessee, Belmont University.

There are all kinds of sin in the world, but if you are around the right kinds of people, that sin can become less and less. As I said earlier, "Those without sin cast the first stone. So everyone has sinned. The Bible says we all fall short of the glory of God, but with Christ, learning and growing in Him, that sin becomes less and less.

Jesus take the wheel that when life really gets good that when you see the rewards and blessing in your life. That's when you see the bigger moon, stars and sunshine, they seem brighter. That's when the flowers seem to blossom a little bigger and brighter. That's what so bright about the word, captivating who Christ is, not just the desire for an outward beauty, but more a desire to be captivating in the depths of who you are. Cinderella is beautiful, yes, but she is also good. Her outward beauty would be hollow were it not for the beauty of her heart. In The Sound of Music, the countess has Maria beat in the looks department and they both know it. But Maria has a rare beautiful depth of spirit. She has the capacity to love snowflakes on kittens, and mean-spirited children. She sees the handiwork of God in music and laughter and climbing trees. Her soul is alive and we are drawn to her.

Men also long for adventure. Boys love to climb, jump, play ball, see how fast they can ride their bikes. Just look in your yard or garage. Adventure is a deeply spiritual longing in the heart of every man. You can find that life—if you are willing to embark on a great adventure.

What a comfort to know that this universe we live in is relational at its core. God is a tenderhearted God who yearns for relationship with us.

Remember the story of Martha and Mary? Mary chose God. Jesus said that is what He wanted. "Mary has chosen what is better." (Luke 10:42) "She chose me."

Chapter 3

A Ride to a Sunset

Let's take another ride,
a ride to a beautiful sunset.

I ride to a soccer game with some friends. When we get to the soccer game, around half-time, I noticed this sunset that—well there was just no other way to describe it—beautiful! I kept looking and looking at it. I forgot about the soccer game. The game was almost over and the score was tied before I realized that I wasn't paying attention to it.

The sunset that God had made won my heart—total peace—total beauty. Then I thought about God and His sending His Son to die on the cross to save world so we may have life. What is that had never happened? Then I thought there was not need to think like that because it did happen.

Christ died on the cross so we may have life. A normal little boy who became a carpenter who grew up, then died on the cross and rose again so we may have life.

What an amazing story, a real story, and a story that makes your life here so important. Think about that. You know you are not going to live on earth forever. Sooner or later, you will die. You see, life spent here on earth is for just a little while, but life that this will be forever, forever, and forever. This is not because I said so, but because the Bible tells me so. There is heaven and there is hell, and both places are real. If you have Christ living in you, you will know it. You will know it by the way you live—by your actions, by sharing it, telling other people about it, and, yes by going to church.

Yes, God wants you to make a public confession of your faith, that you believe Jesus is the Christ, the Son of the living God, you accept Him as your Lord and Savior, and being baptized secures your salvation. As I said earlier, Acts 2:38 tells you to do that and you will be given the gift of the Holy Spirit. In Christ, there is life. Without Christ, life really does not have any meaning.

I remember sitting at a basketball game around

Christmas time, and the team that my son was playing on lost. After the game was over, one of the players from the winning team pulled both teams together to have prayer. Before he had prayed, my son asked him if he was a Christian, and the boy said, "Yes, do you want to pray with me?

Together they pulled both teams together and had prayer after the game was over. I thought that's all that really matters—that we have Christ. What a role model! That kid has a purpose in life and that kid just happens to be on a state championship basketball team. Even in a basketball game, life has a purpose.

One of my favorite Bible verses is Philippians 4:13 KJV. "I can do all things through Christ who strengthens me." In Christ, we can do all things, not just some things. I can make life different. In Him, I can make life better. In Him, my life on earth has a purpose. It has a meaning. One thing I want to do is share my faith with you. Why? Because I want to I want to share my heart with you, I want to grow and grow in Christ.

Chapter 4

Say Yes to God

No one's ever seen or heard anything like this, ever so much as imagined anything quite like it, what God has arranged for those who love him. I Cor.2:9. God prearranged and paid for you to have and enjoy life before you ever showed up on planet earth. Then He sent the Holy Spirit to guide us into all truth and blessing He wants you to have. The key to receiving is simply obedience. When we don't okay God's promptings, we get off track and fail to enjoy all the good things He has in mind for you. Don't let the devil trick you into losing out on God's superabundance because of disobedience.

By sowing seeds of prompt obedience, divine blessings will overtake you. Radical, outrageous, obedience will bring radical, outrageous blessings. Obeying God during the day helps us sleep good at night. Overcome fear with faith. "God has not given us a spirit of fear, but of power and of love, of a sound mind. " 2 Timothy 1:7 NKJV

Have you ever thought of how great it would be if you could live with ever having to deal with fear? Of course, there are healthy fears that alert you to danger in time to avoid it, and these are good because they protect you. But there are many other fears Satan tries to put on you that should not be legitimate concerns. They are false evidence, appearing real, and they are intended to keep you from having power, love and the sound mind God wants you to have.

Fear is a spirit that must be confronted head on—it will not just go away. But God has given you the power to boldly confront your fear and break its hold on your life. So when fear knocks on your door, send faith to answer. Let God be God. For who has known or understood the mind (the counsels and purposes of the Lord so as to guide and instruct Him and give Him knowledge. I Cor. 2:16

It is not our job to give God guidance, counsel or direction. It is our job to listen to God and let Him tell us what is going on and what you are to do about it—leaving the rest to Him to work out according to His knowledge and will, not ours.

God is God—and we are not. We need to recognize that truth and simply trust yourself to Him because He is greater than we are in every way. We are created in His image, But He is still above and beyond us. His thoughts and ways are higher than ours. So listen to God today or tonight, be obedient to Him and He will teach us His way. Cast off your care, releasing the weight of all your burdens, and at night, you sleep peacefully.

Stay in balance with God. Stability is maturity. To grow up in God is to come to the place where you can be content no matter what your situation or circumstances may be because you are rooted and grounded, not in things, but in the Lord.

Paul was emotionally and spiritually mature because he knew whatever state he was in would pass. He had learned the secret of facing every situation of life, whether good or bad. God wants to bless you and use you as a vessel through which His Holy Spirit can work. But in order for that to happen, we must learn how to handle both the good times and the bad. That is why it is so important to remember that whatever comes your way, "This, too, shall pass." The good times and the bad never last forever, but through Christ, we can handle either with joy and stability.

Philippians 4:11 says: "I have learned to be content, satisfied to the point where I am, (not disturbed or disquieted) in what state I am."

Just remember we are just passing through this world. When the devil says, "You're trapped," boldly say to him, "Wrong, I'm just passing through." Shadrach, Meshach, and Abednego were cast into the fiery furnace, but God brought them safely through the fire. (See Daniel 3) Complicated lot that we are, where on earth would we be without Jesus? His Spirit to fill us with love, joy, peace, patience, goodness, kindness, gentleness, faithfulness, and self control?

As time moves on, we have to encourage ourselves in the Lord. In I Samuel 30:6, David was greatly distressed, for the men spoke of stoning him because the souls of the them all were bitterly grieved, each man for his sons and daughters, but David encouraged them and strengthened himself in the Lord, his God.

When David found himself in a seemingly hopeless situation with no one to support him, he encouraged and strengthened himself in the Lord. Later on that situation was totally turned around (See 1 Samuel 30:1-20).

If you don't believe in yourself who is going to? God believes in you, and it is a good thing, too; otherwise, you might never make any progress. You cannot always wait for someone else to come along and encourage you to be all you can be. Confidence is something you decide to have. You learn about God—about His love, His way, and His word—then ultimately you must decide whether you believe it or not. You will not go forward until you decide to believe in God and yourself.

You must have no regrets. Regret is ruining the lives of countless people by stealing their joy. Certainly, you have things you wish you had done differently, but there is not sense becoming burdened with regret over something you have no power to change. You need to understand this is the way the devil works. God will warn you so you can change your mind before you make a mistake. Satan waits until it's too late, when you can o longer do anything about it, and then tries to heap regret and condemnation up you. Don't allow Satan to steal from you any longer. Ask God for forgiveness if you haven't already, and leave your regrets in the past. 2 Corinthians 7:10.

For Godly grief and the paid God is permitted to direct, produce a repentance that leads and contributes to salvation, and deliverance from evil, and it never brings regret. However, worldly grief (the hopeless sorrow that is characteristic of the pagan world) is deadly (breeding and ending in death).

In the end, you can't choose to lose on this ride of faith. All of us become disappointed when we have plans that fail, hopes that don't materialize, and goals that are not reached. When this continues for a while, we become discouraged, a condition that can lead to depression, if not handled properly.

When you get discouraged, you must make a decision to adapt and adjust to take a new approach, to just keep going despite your feelings, that when you must remember the Greater One resides within you and decide you won't let discouragement keep you from realizing your dreams and goals.

When you feel discouraged, it is sometimes difficult to be positive. That's when you must rise above the discouragement through Him who lives in you. He is always available to help you find renewed direction and hope. I always say, "When you're discouraged, get encouraged, and when you're disappointed get reappointed.

There is a time for everything. To everything there is a season, and a time for every matter or purpose under heaven. Ecclesiastes 3:1

If it seems you have been struggling forever with negative things in your life, don't despair. There is a time and season for everything, and bad things ultimately give way to better things.

Even the good things going on in your life may not stay exactly the same because things are always changing. Sometimes changes are exciting... and sometimes they are difficult. But Jesus never changes—and as long as you keep your eyes on Him, you will make it through the changes in your life and continue growing. Be careful not to get too attached people, places, positions, or things, but always be free to move with the Spirit. Let go of what lies behind and press on to what lies ahead. See Philippians 3:13-14. Reach toward the new horizon God has for you. You will be glad you did.

"Blessed assurance, Jesus is mine." That is so true.

In Christ, we have it all. Without Christ, we have nothing.

"I love to tell the story" because I know it is true of Jesus and His love. In His mansion, bright and beautiful, he will make room for you. Soon the pearly gates will open for us.

"Trust in Jesus." Make sure you trust Him more and more. How precious is that! He walks with you and talks with you. Don't reject Him, and He will tell you that you are His own.

Are you "washed in the blood of the lamb"? Be washed in the blood of the lamb, and when this life is over, we will fly away (glory!). Just a few more weary days then we will fly away. You see your friend is in Jesus. If there is trouble, don't be discouraged, take it to the Lord in prayer.

You're "standing on the promises of Christ your Savior." "Turn your eyes upon Jesus. Look full in His wonderful face and the things of this earth will be strangely dim in the light of His glory and grace." See your leaning on the everlasting One.

"On a hill far away stood an old rugged cross." "Cherish that old rugged cross and exchange it someday for a crown."

(Previous quotes were taken from a few words from old gospel hymns.)

How great is that? When I see the stars, I thank Him, great that He is. All this does not end with a slow ride in a hearse, and one day I want to stroll through heaven with you.

My prayer is that whoever gets this book in their hands, that they will put it to work for God's glory. If you are in Christ, you can somehow plant a seed or a garden. If you are away from Christ, I pray that you will accept Christ as your personal Savior.

Still growing in Him.

Love in Christ

Karen Belcher

www.ingramcontent.com/pod-product-compliance
Ingram Content Group UK Ltd.
Pitfield, Milton Keynes, MK11 3LW, UK
UKHW040020200726
13854UKWH00001B/281

9 781412 086646